NOTORIOUS AMERICANS AND THEIR TIMES

Aaron BURR
and the Young Nation

by

W. SCOTT INGRAM

BLACKBIRCH PRESS

THOMSON

GALE

Detroit • New York • San Diego • San Francisco
Boston • New Haven, Conn. • Waterville, Maine
London • Munich

Published by Blackbirch Press
10911 Technology Place
San Diego, CA 92127
Web site: http://www.gale.com/blackbirch
e-mail: customerservice@gale.com

© 2002 by Blackbirch Press,
an imprint of The Gale Group

Printed in the United States

10 9 8 7 6 5 4 3 2 1

Photo credits:
Cover, back cover, pages 10-11, 12-13, 21, 30, 32, 33, 34, 36, 37, 38, 39, 42, 44-45, 46-47, 48, 51, 56-57, 58-59, 83, 87, 93 © North Wind Picture Archive; page 4 © National Portrait Gallery, Smithsonian Institute; pages 18-19, 25, 27, 52, 62, 66, 68, 69, 70, 72, 74, 79, 82, 84, 85, 94, 99, 100 © Dover Publications; pages 20, 28, 63, 75, 100 © The Library of Congress; pages 24, 96 © CORBIS; page 26 © Litchfield Historical Society; page 55 © Bureau of Engraving and Printing

Library of Congress Cataloging-in-Publication Data

Ingram, Scott (William Scott)
Aaron Burr and The Young Nation / by W. Scott Ingram.
        p. cm. - (Notorious Americans and Their Times)
Includes index.
Summary: Discusses the life of Aaron Burr and his duel with Alexander Hamilton.
        ISBN 1-56711-250-1 (Hardcover : alk. paper)
1. Burr, Aaron, 1756-1836—Juvenile literature. 2.Vice-Presidents—United States-Biography—Juvenile literature. 3. Burr—Hamilton Duel, Weehawken, N.J., 1804-Juvenile literature. 4. Burr Conspiracy, 1805-1807—Juvenile literature. 5. Soldiers—United States-Biography—Juvenile literature. 6. United States-History—Revolution, 1775-1783-Biography—Juvenile literature.
[1. Burr, Aaron, 1756-1836. 2. Vice-Presidents. 3. Burr—Hamilton Duel, Weehawken, N.J., 1804.] 1. Title. II. Series.
E302.6.B9 154 2002
973.4161092—dc21   2001005814

TABLE OF CONTENTS

Mist rose in swirling columns from the Hudson River early on the morning of July 11, 1804. At the southern tip of Manhattan, in New York City, Aaron Burr stepped into a rowboat, dressed in a wrinkled silk suit he had slept in. Burr, 48, was a short man, about 5 feet 6 inches tall, with thinning black hair and intense brown eyes. He sat in the stern of the boat as his assistant rowed across the river to New Jersey. They stopped beneath a rock ledge known as Weehawken Heights, an outcropping about 10 feet wide and 40 feet long, slightly above the water line.

Aaron Burr served as vice president under Thomas Jefferson.

A short time later, Alexander Hamilton, 49, arrived by boat from Manhattan, just as Burr had. Accompanying Hamilton were his assistant and his personal physician. Like Burr, Hamilton was a short man, about 5 feet 7 inches tall. He had a fair complexion with bright blue eyes and dark red hair.

Bitter Rivals

The two parties climbed up onto the ledge slightly after 7:00 A.M. and began clearing brush from the rocky surface. Soon, the area was cleared, and the men gathered in the middle of the heights.

Burr and Hamilton had known each other since both had served under George Washington during the American Revolution. Bitter political and personal enemies, the two men were successful lawyers in New York City. Now, nearly thirty years after they fought for American freedom, they came to settle differences that words could not resolve.

They traveled to this out-of-the-way location because they planned to duel with pistols at ten paces. Dueling was illegal in New York and most other states, and therefore had to be kept secret.

Alexander Hamilton was a bitter enemy of Aaron Burr.

According to the long-established rules of dueling, Hamilton had the choice of weapons because Burr had challenged him to the duel. Hamilton's assistant stepped forward and opened a case that held two highly decorated pistols. Burr recognized the guns. In a duel with Hamilton's brother-in-law several years earlier, a bullet from one had shot a button off his coat. Hamilton, too, knew the weapons. His own son had been killed by one of the pistols four years earlier, during a duel to defend his father's honor.

Those close to both men were saddened but not surprised that their long rivalry had led to this violent culmination. Hamilton was an opinionated and outspoken man who had called Burr "unprincipled" and "beyond redemption." Burr had written to Hamilton, asking him to apologize for his insults. Hamilton had refused, saying that an apology would be a lie because everything he had said about Burr was true. Finally, the hot-tempered Burr felt he had no choice. He challenged Hamilton to an "interview" —the code word for a duel.

After each man selected his weapon, the assistants returned to their boats. The doctor turned his back on

Burr and Hamilton. If there was an investigation of the event, the men wanted to able to testify truthfully that they had seen nothing.

Holding their guns, Burr and Hamilton paced off ten steps, putting each at the edge of the rocky outcropping. The smooth bore pistol each man held fired a large round ball. In those days, before gun barrels were grooved, or rifled, weapons were wildly inaccurate. A great deal of force, more than twenty pounds, was required to pull the trigger of a pistol. In fact, although dueling was illegal, it was rarely deadly. Most "interviews" ended when both parties had fired their weapons and either missed their opponents or caused a slight flesh wound.

No "Ill Will"

As Hamilton and Burr paced off their distance, Burr had no way of knowing that Hamilton had no intention of shooting him. The night before, Hamilton had written in a letter that he felt no personal "ill will" toward Burr, only toward his political beliefs. He expressed regret that their rivalry had resulted

Aaron Burr fires on Alexander Hamilton during their famous duel in New Jersey, July 1804.

in a duel and spelled out his decision to "throw away my first fire"—in other words, to miss on purpose.

All that remained was the shooting. Under dueling rules, Hamilton had the first shot, since it was he who had been challenged. Hamilton asked Burr for a slight delay while he put on his eyeglasses and aimed at several imaginary targets. He then nodded.

A shot rang out. True to his word, Hamilton fired at a spot high in a tree over Burr's head. Burr raised his weapon and aimed. In later years, he claimed that he meant only to wound Hamilton in the side. Unfortunately for Hamilton—and in the end for Burr as well—the ball from Burr's pistol struck Hamilton about four inches above his right hip. The large projectile ripped a two-inch hole in Hamilton's flesh. It then cracked his rib cage, bounced off the bone and passed through his liver and diaphragm. The deadly metal finally lodged in Hamilton's spine.

Even with modern medicine, it is unlikely that Hamilton could have survived such a devastating injury. If he had, he would have most likely been paralyzed. Hamilton fell to ground. When the doctor rushed to his side, Hamilton calmly said, "This is a

After the duel, assistants tended to a mortally wounded Alexander Hamilton.

mortal wound." He lost consciousness and died the next day.

Burr, meanwhile, realized that this was a terrible turn of events and tried to rush to Hamilton. His assistant, however, had hurried up to the ledge after the shots were fired. He held Burr back, then forced him off the ledge and into the boat to flee back across the Hudson.

One historian called the duel between Burr and Hamilton "the most dramatic moment in the early politics of the Union." On the morning the men met in Weehawken Heights, Hamilton and Burr were two of the most well-known leaders in the new nation. Hamilton had been the first secretary of the treasury under Washington. He had been one of the architects of the U.S. Constitution. Only four years earlier, Hamilton had served as the commanding general of the U.S. Army. That such a man would die in a duel was sickening to many Americans. That the man who killed him was Aaron Burr was even worse: Burr was the vice president of the United States.

A "New Benedict Arnold"

The vice president was quickly vilified in the press. Within days after Hamilton's death, newspapers claimed that Burr had murdered Hamilton in cold blood. The vice president was compared to Benedict Arnold, the notorious Revolutionary War traitor. One paper reported that Burr had worn a special bulletproof suit. Another stated that Burr had only expressed regret that he had not killed Hamilton instantly with a bullet to the heart.

An illustration of the time showed Burr and several accomplices hiding behind shrubs to ambush Hamilton. Verse under the illustration read:

O Burr, O Burr, what hast thou done?

Thou has shooted dead great Hamilton.

You hid behind a bunch of thistle

And shooted him dead with a great hoss pistol.

When it came time to mourn the loss of an American national icon, the nation rose to the occasion. Hamilton's funeral was one of the most extravagant in the history of early America. His coffin was pulled down Broadway in New York City. The coffin was trailed by his gray horse, with Hamilton's riding boots placed backward in the stirrups. Following the horse were Hamilton's wife and seven surviving children. Behind them were bank presidents, military officers, and the entire faculty and student body of Columbia College, where Hamilton had studied before the Revolution. Several hundred other mourners followed the procession. This show of support—the hundreds who were personal friends and admirers of Hamilton marching together in public—only made Burr's disgraceful act more despicable.

While Hamilton was receiving a hero's memorial, Burr had fled the city in disgrace. He had traveled all the way to the wilds of Georgia to remain in seclusion. Burr was soon out of office, and there is little argument among historians that his actions during the years that followed marked him as a traitor and made him one of the most notorious characters in American history.

Chapter 2

RUMBLINGS OF REBELLION: THE BRILLIANT STUDENT

Most people who study the early history of the United States know the names of people such as George Washington, Thomas Jefferson, and Alexander Hamilton. Those men, along with many others, created a nation from thirteen colonies more than two hundred years ago. Few people who have studied the history of the early United States, however, know much about Aaron Burr. Like

Washington, Jefferson, Hamilton, and others, Burr fought for the freedom of the young nation. But unlike those statesman, Burr's name has been forgotten. And unlike the men who are honored for their contribution to the cause of freedom, Aaron Burr brought dishonor to himself. If his plans had succeeded, the United States today might be a very different country.

A Young Orphan

Aaron Burr was born in Newark, New Jersey, in 1756. A sister, Sally, had been born two years before. His father, also named Aaron, was the president of the College of New Jersey. When Aaron was an infant, the college moved to Princeton, New Jersey, and was renamed after the town. The elder Aaron was a professor as well as president. He taught mathematics, Greek, and Latin.

The senior Aaron Burr was a college president and professor.

Burr's mother, Esther Edwards Burr, was the daughter of one of colonial America's most famous religious leaders, Jonathan Edwards. Edwards was well known for his stern moral values, his fiery sermons, and strict religious beliefs.

Young Aaron and his sister had little chance to know their parents. Their father died from a fever in 1757. Their mother, Esther, died of smallpox less than a year later. Esther's parents—Sally and Aaron's grandparents

Jonathan Edwards, Aaron Burr's grandfather, was a well known religious leader.

—died shortly thereafter. Thus, at the young ages of four and two, orphans Sally and Aaron were sent to live with their uncle, Timothy Edwards, in nearby Elizabethtown, New Jersey.

Colonies at War

During the difficult first years of Aaron's life, the British colonies also faced an uncertain future. In the middle 1700s, the colonies did not extend beyond the Appalachian Mountains. The huge area west of those mountains, from western Pennsylvania to the Ohio River Valley and the northern Great Lakes south down the Mississippi River, was a wilderness claimed by

This map shows early French and British settlements in North America.

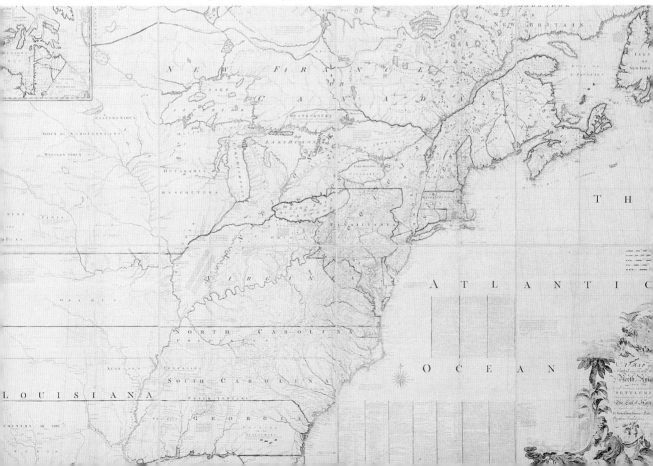

During the 1700s, cities in the British colonies began to grow. This engraving shows colonists dealing with a fabric merchant.

France. As the population of the British colonies began to grow, settlers moved into the areas west of the Appalachians toward the Ohio River Valley. As a result, both Great Britain and France began to build forts in these areas to strengthen their claims to the wide open land.

In 1754, two years before Aaron Burr was born, the British governor of Virginia sent a young militia officer named George Washington into a French region near the modern city of Pittsburgh, Pennsylvania. Washington carried a letter from the British governor demanding that the French leave the area. A series of battles followed, one of which Washington won and another in which he was defeated. These conflicts were the first battles of what came to be known as the French and Indian War.

War was not officially declared until two years later, the year Aaron Burr was born. For the next seven years, battles between British forces and French troops, aided by Native American tribes, took place from Nova Scotia, Canada, to the Ohio River Valley. More than 10,000 British troops came to the colonies to fight. Finally, in 1763, the French signed the Treaty of Paris, which gave Great Britain control of all of North America east of the Mississippi River.

The new land made Great Britain one of the most powerful nations in the world. But the cost of the war, and the cost of supporting troops in the colonies, was extremely high. As a result, British leaders passed a number of tax laws to force colonists to pay their share of the war's expenses. These increasingly high taxes pushed the colonies to the revolt that led to the American Revolution.

A Brief and Difficult Childhood

Young Aaron and his sister were not old enough to understand the conflicts between colonies and countries. As a child, Aaron was a "dirty, noisy boy, sly and mischievous," according to his memoirs. This sort of behavior did not meet his uncle's approval, and Aaron was often, as he later put it, "beaten like a sack" by Edwards. Aaron was so unhappy living with his uncle that he twice tried to run away to sea. The only time that Aaron was happy was when he was studying under the supervision of his tutor. In those days, there were no public schools, and education was available only to the wealthiest families. Aaron's tutor was a young Princeton graduate named Tapping Reeve. Aaron remained friends with Reeve throughout his life, and his sister Sally eventually married Reeve.

Aaron was an exceptionally good student—so good, in fact, that he applied for admission to

Princeton University when he was only eleven years old. He was rejected because of his age, but two years later he was accepted. Aaron was so advanced that he was placed in the second-year class at age 13 in 1769.

When he was only 13 years old, Aaron Burr entered Princeton University.

While a student at Princeton, Aaron was invited to become a member of Cliosophic Society, a debating club. The main topics of debate during those years were the same subjects on the minds of many colonists—unfair taxation and British control. Even as a young teenager, Aaron was a powerful speaker who was able to persuade others to accept his beliefs. Like many students, including his classmate, future president James Madison, Aaron deeply resented the power that Great Britain exercised over the colonies. He spoke out often against Britain's king and against the idea of royalty.

Future president James Madison was a classmate of Burr's at Princeton.

Young Aaron Burr graduated from Princeton at age 16 in 1772. Because many of the men in his family had been ministers, Aaron began religious studies in the fall of 1773. He soon found that his personal

Aaron Burr attended the Litchfield Law School, which was run by his brother-in-law, Tapping Reeve.

beliefs did not agree with the religious principles he was being taught. He left theology school, and chose instead to study law.

Attending law school was not a simple matter in the 1700s. In fact, the first university school of law was not established until 1779 at the College of William and Mary in Virginia. As it happened, however, Aaron's former tutor, Tapping Reeve, moved to Litchfield, Connecticut, soon after marrying Burr's sister, Sally, in 1773. In Litchfield, Reeve established a private school of law—and his new brother-in-law, Aaron, became one of the first students. Reeve's newly established school soon gained a solid reputation for giving students a thorough knowledge of law as well as a spirit of independence.

TAPPING REEVE: A LIFETIME IN LAW

Tapping Reeve was born on Long Island, New York, in 1744. By the time of his death in 1823, he had become one of the most widely respected law teachers in America. Reeve, who tutored young Aaron Burr, moved to Hartford, Connecticut, in the early 1770s to work as a law clerk. After marrying Sally Burr in 1773, he moved to Litchfield, Connecticut, and began giving law classes in his office. By 1784, Reeve had so many students that he built a cottage next to his office. This became known as the Litchfield Law School.

Reeve was the only teacher at the school until 1798, when he took a seat on the Connecticut Supreme Court. Reeve asked one of his students, James Gould, to help him in the management and education at the school. Reeve and

Tapping Reeve

Gould drew students from almost every part of the United States to study law in their unheated, one-room school-house. Students at Litchfield Law School received classroom instruction and were able to participate in practice courtroom sessions under the supervision of Reeve and Gould.

Litchfield Law School trained some of the most famous men in the early nineteenth century. In addition to Aaron Burr, students included Senator John C. Calhoun, educator Horace Mann, author Herman Melville, and wordsmith Noah Webster. More than 1,000 students graduated from the school, including sixteen U.S. senators, fifty congressmen, two justices of the U.S. Supreme Court, ten governors, and five cabinet officers. The school closed in 1833.

Paul Revere rode through the Massachusetts countryside on April 18, 1775, to alert colonists that British soldiers were advancing toward them.

Aaron's law studies were interrupted by the events of April 1775. That month, news of battles between colonists and British troops at Lexington and Concord in Massachusetts instantly spread through the colonies. Like many other colonists, 19-year-old Aaron Burr viewed these clashes as a call to duty.

Chapter 3

THE REVOLUTION BEGINS
A YOUNG MAN AT WAR

$\mathcal{I}$t is not surprising that Aaron Burr strongly supported the cause of independence. He was a rebellious child who ran away from the strict rules of his uncle. As a 13-year-old college student, he was forced to compete with students who were much older, an experience that fostered Burr's lifelong core of self-confidence and independence. His decision to join the anti-royalty Cliosophic Society at age 15 also shows that he favored the ideal of independence.

For a teenager such as Burr, growing up in the 1760s and 1770s offered an exciting chance to put beliefs into action. By the time he became a law student in 1774, the colonies had suffered for more than ten years under harsh taxation and strict laws from the British government.

Between 1763 and 1773, the British Parliament passed tax laws to raise money to pay for the debts resulting from the French and Indian War. The Parliament also passed the Quartering Act, which required colonists to provide food, shelter, and supplies for 10,000 British troops stationed in the colonies. Of all the acts passed by the British, however, the Stamp Act of 1765 was the law that angered colonists the most.

Under the Stamp Act, colonists were required to pay a tax on most printed goods—newspapers, legal records, advertisements, and even playing cards. Colonists claimed this tax had been passed by Parliament without colonial participation. It was, in the words of the colonies' famous rallying cry, "taxation without representation." The protests of the colonists, as well as their refusal to pay the taxes in many cases, led Parliament to repeal the Stamp Act

The British Parliament passed tax laws that infuriated the colonists.

THE REVOLUTION BEGINS

In 1770, British troops fired on colonists in what became known as the Boston Massacre.

in 1766. This repeal, however, did not end the practice of passing tax laws and other legislation without colonists' representation.

The disagreements became violent in 1770, when British troops fired on a crowd of colonists in Boston. The crowd had initially gathered to protest the practice of trying colonists before a British judge

Colonists marched in New York and other cities to protest the Stamp Act.

rather than a colonial jury. Five colonists were killed in what became known as the "Boston Massacre." Boston was again the scene of protest in 1773 when a group of colonists disguised as Native Americans threw several hundred pounds of British tea into Boston Harbor. This action, known as the "Boston Tea Party," set in motion a chain of events that soon led to the American Revolution.

After the Boston Tea Party, the British closed the port of Boston and took away most of the Massachusetts colony's right to govern itself. This action led to a meeting of colonial delegates in September 1774—around the same time that Aaron Burr was beginning law school in Litchfield. The delegates demanded that Britain open Boston Harbor and withdraw its military. They agreed among themselves to meet again the following summer if their demands were not met.

Before that meeting could take place, however, the American Revolution began in April 1775. The British military governor of Massachusetts sent troops out from Boston to seize weapons from colonists known as the Minutemen, citizens who had trained to take up arms against the British.

In 1773, colonists dumped shipments of tea into Boston Harbor to protest the tea tax.

On April 19, two battles were fought at Lexington and Concord. News of the battles traveled rapidly throughout the colonies.

From Cambridge to Quebec

By July 1775, 19-year-old Burr was in Boston, hoping to join the fight for independence. As it happened, another American who would later

Colonial soldiers, known as Minutemen, prepare to fight.

General George Washington was responsible for creating a regular army in the early days of the Revolution.

become notorious was also in Boston. His name was Benedict Arnold. At that time, Arnold was a colonial officer who supported the American cause. In late summer 1775, Arnold met in Boston with General George Washington, the Virginia farmer who had become well known during the French and Indian War. Washington, who was trying to build a regular army from the various groups of Minutemen and other colonists, had a plan to invade Canada. He felt that attacking Quebec, the capital of Canada, would force the British to defend areas far from the colonies. This strategy would allow him more time to train a fighting force. Arnold volunteered to lead troops across the wilderness of Maine and attack Quebec. Burr, hoping for action, volunteered to join Arnold's force

Benedict Arnold

Burr was a member of the American forces that attacked Quebec in December 1775.

AARON BURR AND THE YOUNG NATION

of more than 1,000 colonists. Burr's family was horrified that the small, untrained teenager would attempt such a strenuous and dangerous mission. Young Burr, however, was idealistic and determined to prove his devotion to the cause of liberty. Arnold's force left Boston in September 1775.

The troops faced problems right away. Few maps of Maine existed, and those that did were not accurate. The distance the troops had to travel was more than twice what they had planned. By the third week, Arnold's troops were starving. The men cooked and ate a dog that had come into camp. They were forced to eat soap, leather pouches, and candles. By the time Arnold's force reached Quebec, death and desertion had reduced the force to fewer than 700 men. One of those men was Burr. In fact, the young soldier had handled the challenge so well that he was promoted to captain.

After several weeks of rest in the frigid area outside of Quebec, the Americans attacked the city on December 31, 1775. As they attacked, a blinding snowstorm swirled around them. Burr was among a squad of men who were attempting to enter the city when their group was caught in cannon fire. When the smoke cleared, only Burr and a Native American guide were left alive. The attack was a total failure, and American soldiers fled from the battleground.

An Officer in Action

It took Burr several months to make his way back to the colonies. His bravery, however, had won wide respect among those who had fought with him. In May 1776, Burr was offered a position as a major on the staff of General Washington.

Although it was an honor to serve under the commander of colonial forces, Burr was not impressed by Washington. The two men could not have been more different. The physical contrast between the two was startling. Washington, a rough-looking man with a pockmarked face, stood nearly 6 feet, 4 inches tall and weighed well over 200 pounds. Burr was a slight, smooth-faced youth, barely 5 feet, 6 inches tall.

There were greater differences between the two, however, than just appearance. Burr was a highly educated, cultured student of military history. He saw Washington as an uneducated Indian fighter with little military training.

Burr's dissatisfaction soon led him to ask for a transfer. He was replaced by another slight young officer who had gained a reputation as a strong leader. His name was Alexander Hamilton. Washington and Hamilton formed a close relationship that lasted for almost twenty-five years.

F.C. YOHN

Burr remained in New York through 1776 and 1777, fighting British troops in a number of small battles. The Redcoats (British soldiers), however, proved superior during most of the fighting around New York and New Jersey. By the winter of 1777-1778, the British controlled Philadelphia. Burr, along with much of the colonial army, was forced to spend a brutal winter at Valley Forge. Unlike many colonial soldiers, Burr did not complain about the hardships during that difficult time. For a young man who had walked across Maine and suffered the bitter cold of Quebec, Valley Forge was bearable.

By February 1778, the tide of the war was beginning to change. A new alliance between American colonists and the French tipped the balance of power against British interests. On February 6, representatives from the colonies and France signed two treaties in Paris. The first was the Treaty of Amity and Commerce, the second was the Treaty of Alliance. With the signing of these documents, both countries pledged to fight until American independence was won. Both countries also agreed that neither would sign any truce with Britain without the other's consent.

American forces who spent the winter of 1777-1778 at Valley Forge endured brutal conditions.

France also formally recognized the United States and became the major source of military supplies for Washington's army. When British ships fired on the French following the signing of the treaties, France officially declared war on Britain. From that point on, the British faced major wars on many fronts. No longer was their conflict only with America—it now involved other countries in Europe. Eventually, Britain was at war with the Spanish and the Dutch, and was forced to fight in the Mediterranean, Africa, India, and the West Indies.

45

In late June 1778, the British forces were ordered to withdraw from Philadelphia to New York. Colonial troops followed the Redcoats, engaging them in the Battle of Monmouth, New Jersey. Burr was in the thick of the fighting on that blistering hot day. He eventually fell during the battle, not to musket balls, but to heat stroke. By autumn, Burr had been fighting almost three years straight, and he requested a leave of absence for health reasons. He returned to active duty in early 1779, commanding defense lines around the Hudson River. His health, however, continued to worsen. In March 1779, Burr resigned from active duty. Washington accepted Burr's resignation with regret, for the small, dark-haired colonel had proven himself to be a fierce and clever fighter.

Burr hoped to return to his law studies. Soon, however, he met a woman who changed the direction of his life once again.

Burr requested a leave of absence from the army soon after the Battle of Monmouth.

48

Chapter 4

After resigning from active duty, Burr remained in the New York City area and carried messages between camps of colonial soldiers. The area around the lower Hudson River was the site of frequent battles between British troops and colonials. In the region, there were also a number of Loyalists—Americans who remained loyal to Britain—as well as some family members of British troops.

After resigning from active duty in 1779, Burr returned to law school.

In late 1780, Burr met Mrs. Theodosia Prevost, widow of a colonel in the British army. Although Prevost was ten years older than the 24-year-old Burr, the two felt an immediate attraction. Burr felt that Prevost was not only charming, but also extremely intelligent. For an educated man like Burr, she was a perfect match—except that she was a good deal older and she had five children.

In an attempt to forget the widow, Burr returned to law school. For the next several years, however, his studies were interrupted by deep depressions that kept him bedridden for weeks. Finally, Burr took his bar examination in Albany, New York, and was admitted to practice in April 1782. He opened a law office in Albany, and in July, married Theodosia Prevost. In his memoirs, Burr says that he was immediately attracted to his wife for her grace and charm and because "she had the truest heart and finest intellect" of any woman he had ever met. In June 1783, Burr's daughter—named Theodosia after her mother—was born in Albany. His extraordinary love for his daughter was one of the most notable aspects of his character.

By 1783, New York was a thriving port city.

Six months after his daughter's birth, Burr moved his family to New York City. New York was then a growing port with a population of more than 22,000. Burr arrived just time to see the British leave—the American Revolution had come to an end.

As the year 1784 began, the colonies were free at last. They were not, however, united. They were, in fact, still like thirteen separate countries. Raising a single army from a group of thirteen individual state militias had been difficult for Washington—though they were all fighting for the same cause, soldiers still felt their loyalty was to their home colony. Many men who grew tired of fighting simply left their posts and returned home. Paying soldiers was not an option. Because there was no national treasury, the paper money issued to troops was little more than an IOU. The great statesman Benjamin Franklin went to Paris during the Revolution to ask for French money to pay colonial soldiers. When he arrived, he found three other ambassadors there from separate colonies also asking for money. Thus, in the mid-1780s, many patriots realized that creating a

Ben Franklin had worked to finance the American Revolution.

nation would require as much determination as the struggle for independence had required.

A Decade of Disagreement

In 1776, most colonists had agreed wholeheartedly with the statement in the Declaration of Independence that all people had the right to "life, liberty, and the pursuit of happiness." That document helped to unite the colonies in a common goal: freedom from England. Once independence had been achieved, however, colonists had many different ideas about governing the new nation. No country before that time had been a democracy. There was no model of a democratic republic to follow. As a result, differences of opinion about the powers that a government should have arose throughout the new United States.

The difficulty in finding a common opinion about government was caused in large measure by differences among the colonies. Some colonies, such as Virginia, were large, with an economy based on agriculture. Others, such as Connecticut, were small and had an economy based on manufacturing and trade. And though colonists in both the North and the South felt strongly about the fight for freedom, that same spirit that drove the colonies to fight for independence made them unwilling surrender their hard-won freedom to any national government.

During the Revolution, the ruling body of the colonies had been known as the Continental Congress. In 1777, that group had approved a governing document known as the Articles of Confederation. This document created a very loose association of colonies. As loose as the confederation was, however, it took until 1781 for all thirteen colonies to ratify, or accept, the document. There was a great deal of disagreement over whose right it was to collect taxes, raise armies, control courts, and issue money. Some said these tasks belonged to each colony individually. Others said those tasks were the role of a central, or federal, government.

By the mid-1780s, it was obvious that the Articles of Confederation were a failure. Colonies owed debts to foreign powers, but had no way to raise money. Trade between the colonies was difficult because each had different currency. No one knew how much New York currency was worth compared to Rhode Island or Delaware currency. There was no way to raise a national army or navy in case the colonies were attacked by a foreign power.

Those problems and others led the colonies to send 55 delegates to the Constitutional Convention of 1787, held at Independence Hall in Philadelphia, the site where the Declaration of Independence had been created only eleven years earlier. The task set before these men was in some ways more challenging than agreeing on the principles of 1776. The delegates

Independence Hall was the site where both the Constitution and the Declaration of Independence were created.

would have to agree on a new form of government that met the needs of colonies large and small, rich and poor, north and south. Among the delegates were future presidents Thomas Jefferson, James Madison, and James Monroe. George Washington was the chairman of the group. One of the New York delegates was Alexander Hamilton. Burr was not nominated as a delegate. Even if he had been, it is unlikely he would have been able to leave his law practice, his new family, or his wife, who had become an invalid by that time.

Eventually, after much bitter argument, the delegates created a Constitution that established the form of democratic government that controls the United States today. The power to govern, the Constitution stated, would be shared by an executive branch and a legislative branch. A judicial branch would review all decisions made by the other two branches.

There was general agreement on the divisions of government, but the debate over the powers of a federal government divided people into two groups. One group became known as the Federalists. These people supported a strong national government that would pass laws, raise armies, operate courts, collect taxes, control trade, and print currency. Many Federalists lived in the Northeast, where trade among colonies and in Europe was important. Among the most extreme Federalists was Hamilton, who wanted the president and senators to be elected for life and the state governors appointed by the president.

The Constitutional Convention was held in Philadelphia's Old State House, later renamed Independence Hall.

On the other side of the debate were those who believed in a weaker central government. These people believed that states should have the power to make the laws that controlled daily life, as well as any powers not granted to the federal government. They wanted a president and a legislature elected by the people (though in those days only white men who owned property could vote). This group was first known as Anti-Federalists, but later became known as "Republicans." The strongest Republican of all was the man from Virginia who wrote the Declaration of Independence—Thomas Jefferson. Jefferson, like many Americans in the agricultural South, was a firm believer in what became known as "states' rights." The people who came to be called "Jeffersonian Republicans" feared that giving a large amount of power to a central government might lead to a loss of individual and states' rights. Even though Jefferson served two terms as president and became a strong supporter of the federal court system, he always referred to Virginia, his home state, as "my country." He was so "state centered" that his tombstone, in fact, does not mention that he was a president of the United States.

Delegates to the Constitutional Convention signed the Constitution in September 1787.

AARON BURR AND THE YOUNG NATION

We the People

of the United States, in order to form a more perfect Union, establish Justice, insure domestic Tranquility, provide for the common defence, promote the general Welfare, and secure the Blessings of Liberty to ourselves and our Posterity, do ordain and establish this Constitution for the United States of America.

Article. I.

Article. II.

Article. III.

Article. IV.

Article. V.

Article. VI.

Article. VII.

done

in Convention by the Unanimous Consent of the States present the Seventeenth Day of September in the Year of our Lord one thousand seven hundred and Eighty seven and of the Independance of the United States of America the Twelfth. In Witness whereof We have hereunto subscribed our Names,

Attest William Jackson Secretary

G⁰. Washington—Presid⁺. and deputy from Virginia

Delaware {
Geo: Read
Gunning Bedford jun
John Dickinson
Richard Bassett
Jaco: Broom
}

James McHenry

Maryland {
Dan of St Thos. Jenifer
}

New Hampshire {
John Langdon
Nicholas Gilman
}

Massachusetts {
Nathaniel Gorham
Rufus King
}

Connecticut {
Wm. Saml. Johnson
Roger Sherman
}

Hamilton and Washington, D.C.

By the time of his death in 1804, Alexander Hamilton's political career had been over for several years. His views of a powerful central government were widely disliked and many people suspected him of being sympathetic to British interests. Few people realized how much Hamilton did to get the new nation on solid economic footing. Even fewer people realized the role Hamilton played in choosing Washington, D.C., as the nation's capital.

Hamilton was a farsighted thinker. When agriculture was a key part of the American economy in the late 1700s, Hamilton saw that the future of the country was in industry. To develop

Alexander Hamilton

into an industrial power, he believed, America would need a powerful centralized economic system. In the years after the Revolution, however, the American economy was in ruins. The war had been paid for largely with bonds—which are basically government IOUs. After the war, because the government could not collect taxes, it could not pay its debts or pay for any national projects.

As the first secretary of the treasury, Hamilton knew that taxes were unpopular but necessary. He developed a plan that would collect taxes to pay the war debts. He also recommended that the federal government take on and pay any debts the states had acquired. Many anti-Federalists argued that this expanded the federal government. Besides, they said, if the debts of states that still owed money were taken on by the federal government, citizens in states that had already paid off their debts would have to pay twice. Instead of reasoning with lawmakers who objected to his debt plan, Hamilton made a trade to get his financial plan approved by Congress. The state that objected most to the sharing of state debts was wealthy Virginia. But Virginians were also unhappy that the location of the federal capital was in the Northeast. Hamilton held a private meeting with Virginia congressman James Madison. The two made a deal: Madison and the Virginians would support Hamilton's plan for taking on state debts. In return, the federal government would support moving the capital to a location on the Potomac River in Virginia. With the support of Virginia, Hamilton's plan was approved

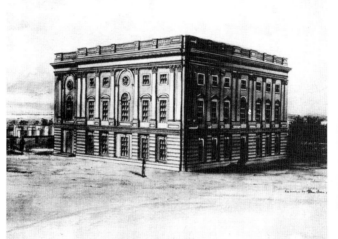

Capital in Washington, 1800

by Congress. Construction of a capital city, called Washington, D.C., began in 1790. In 1800, John Adams became the first president to reside in the capital.

Although he was called a "dictator" and a "would-be king" by his enemies, Hamilton's ability to save the economy of the young nation was a tremendous service to America.

Burr Enters Politics

Throughout the 1780s, while the debate over the form of government took place, Burr built a successful law practice. A lover of parties, he became a well-known figure at social gatherings in New York City. He was referred to as "Colonel" Burr—his Revolutionary War rank—on the society pages of newspapers. Burr's appreciation of the finer things in life kept him in almost constant debt. Nevertheless, his great speaking ability and knowledge of the law brought him many clients. So he somehow managed to support a large family.

Burr had been in New York City for only six months when he was elected to the New York State Assembly. This came as a surprise to him because he had not sought office. He made good use of his time, however, by becoming a strong supporter of a law to abolish slavery in New York. Such a position was quite unusual at this time. The question of slavery was one on which most lawmakers in the late 1700s remained silent. Burr served on a committee to revise the slavery law in the state, but served only one term before returning to his law practice and his invalid wife in New York City.

Burr's chief rival as a New York lawyer was Alexander Hamilton. While they often clashed in court and were on opposite sides of the political fence, the two respected each other. Hamilton was a strong Federalist who believed that a successful nation needed a powerful government. Burr believed more in individual freedom and states' rights.

The First Move into National Politics

After the Constitution was written, it required the approval—called ratification—of two-thirds of the states before it became the law of the nation. That meant approval of eight states in all, because Rhode Island had not sent delegates. Although the two-thirds majority was achieved by 1788, the two largest and wealthiest colonies, New York and Virginia, held out. The delegates knew that without the ratification of those states, the Constitution would have very little value.

During 1788, Hamilton and James Madison—Burr's old Princeton classmate—worked tirelessly to win approval from the state leaders. Madison, a Virginian, was finally able to persuade his fellow Virginians to ratify the document—the state legislature approved it by a narrow margin of 89 to 79.

THE *FEDERALIST PAPERS*

One of the key issues addressed in the *Federalist Papers* was that of the separation of powers guaranteed by the Constitution. In Federalist #51, James Madison discusses the need for checks and balances:

"But the great security against a gradual concentration of the several powers in the same department, consists in giving to those who administer each department the necessary constitutional means and personal motives to resist encroachments of the others. . . . Ambition must be made to counteract ambition. . . . It may be a reflection on human nature, that such devices should be necessary to control the abuses of government. But what is government itself, but the greatest of all reflections on human nature? If men were angels, no government would be necessary. If angels were to govern men, neither external nor internal controls on government would be necessary. In framing a government which is to be administered by men over men, the great difficulty lies in this: you must first enable the government to control the governed;

James Madison

and in the next place oblige it to control itself. "

Opponents of the Constitution were concerned that a president might try to rule as a dictator and instead wanted several persons in the executive branch of government rather than just one. In Federalist #70, Alexander Hamilton explains the potential pitfalls of such a system:

Alexander Hamilton

"Wherever two or more persons are engaged in any common enterprise or pursuit, there is always danger of difference of opinion. If it be a public trust or office, in which they are clothed with equal dignity and authority, there is peculiar danger of personal emulation and even animosity. From either, and especially from all these causes, the most bitter dissensions are apt to spring. Whenever these happen, they lessen the respectability, weaken the authority, and distract the plans and operation of those whom they divide."

John Jay

Madison and Hamilton next turned their attention to New York. Together with delegate John Jay, the three men wrote more than eighty newspaper articles under the pen name "Publius." Those writings became known as the *Federalist Papers*.

The *Federalist Papers* made the argument for a strong central—or federal—government. Such a government, the articles claimed, was needed in a nation that encompassed a large geographical area and had a population of immigrants from various countries and social levels. A central power would allow all regions and all people a voice in the way their country was governed. The *Federalist Papers*

George Washington

convinced many dubious state lawmakers that their approval of the Constitution had been a wise decision. More importantly, the work persuaded the New York assembly to ratify the Constitution—although by an even narrower vote than Virginia's, 30 to 27.

The success of the *Federalist Papers* led to future success for the three authors. James Madison—who had done most of the writing—became known as the "Father of the Constitution." He also was elected the fourth president of the United States. John Jay went on to become the first chief justice of the U.S. Supreme Court. Hamilton became the first secretary of the treasury.

In 1789, before all the states had ratified the Constitution, George Washington was elected as the nation's first president. He took office in New York City, the nation's first capital city. Washington was a presidential choice that satisfied all parties. He was a military hero, and possibly the one person in the new nation who was above politics. Though he was the first democratically elected leader of a nation that rejected monarchy, there was some pageantry surrounding the new president. The president was driven around New York City in a yellow coach pulled by six white horses. On the occasions when he rode a horse, his saddle was strapped over a leopard skin blanket.

New York Governor George Clinton (pictured) appointed Burr State attorney general.

Burr also entered the world of politics in 1789, when the governor of New York, George Clinton, appointed him the attorney general of the state—the highest legal position in state government. By 1791, the federal government had undergone great change. The Constitution had been ratified by all thirteen colonies—now called states. Before it was approved, however, ten changes, or amendments, were added.

Philip Schuyler (pictured) was Burr's opponent when Burr ran for the U.S. Senate in 1791.

This "Bill of Rights" guaranteed the freedom of speech, religion, the press, and other rights that are highly valued by Americans today. By that time, the nation's capital had also moved from New York to Philadelphia.

Burr decided to run for the U.S. Senate from New York in 1791. His opponent in the election was Philip Schuyler. Schuyler was an older man, nearing sixty,

Robert Livingston

who had fought in both the French and Indian War and the Revolution. His daughter, Elizabeth, was married to Alexander Hamilton, now the secretary of the treasury. It was this political contest and election that fueled the growing hatred between Burr and Hamilton. Hamilton, of course, supported the election of his father-in-law to the Senate. Hamilton needed support for many of his national economic policies, and Schuyler was a Federalist. Burr had greater sympathy for the Republican cause. He also had the support of New York's powerful Governor Clinton as well as that of Robert Livingston, a wealthy New York politician.

At that time, the political process, like everything else in the United States, was brand-new. Until the mid-1800s, it was actually considered rude for candidates to speak in public and ask for votes. Most campaigning was done through newspapers or other printed material. Burr was among the first people to understand the importance of building a political base of support. He was able to gain the backing of powerful families by promising to advance their interests in the Senate. He was also able to gain the support of less powerful people by promising to guard their individual rights as well. His understanding of the way a political campaign worked in a democracy was years ahead of its time.

Burr won election to the Senate in 1791 and immediately left for Philadelphia. His enthusiasm for politics meant that he soon made as many enemies as friends. He was as likely to vote for his personal interests, or those of his wealthy supporters, as he was for Republican issues. Unlike Washington, who had the reputation for being above politics, Burr operated behind the scenes and chose the position that would personally benefit him the most.

It was in these first years that he was on the national political scene that widespread criticism of Burr took hold. Chief among Burr's critics was Hamilton. He wrote to friends that Burr was "unprincipled both as a public and private man," and that "if he can he will certainly disturb our institutions to secure himself permanent power and wealth."

Burr's term in the Senate was generally unhappy, due largely to the fact that his beloved wife,

Theodosia Burr

Theodosia, died in 1794. He wanted to resign his seat to be with his wife in her final days, but she refused to allow it. After her death, Burr and his daughter, Theodosia, shared their grief and became even more devoted to each other.

Theodosia Burr was eleven at the time of her mother's death. She spoke four languages and played the harp and the piano. Theodosia acquired these skills in an era when the very idea of educating girls at all was shocking. Fewer than fifty percent of American women in 1794 could spell their own names. As he was in other aspects of his life, Burr was ahead of his time regarding the education of his daughter. The fact that he allowed her to skate, dance, and ride a horse was almost too much for proper society to bear. Yet, by age fourteen, Theodosia Burr was considered one of the most charming and cultured young women in America. Many years later, Burr himself would be called one of the first male feminists in the United States.

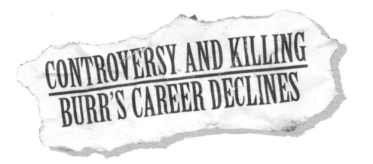

Chapter 5

CONTROVERSY AND KILLING
BURR'S CAREER DECLINES

By 1796, Burr had become one of the best-known politicians in America. Although he had bitter enemies—in Hamilton as well as the second president, John Adams—Burr was popular among the Jeffersonian Republicans, who were mainly middle-class Americans. He became so popular, in fact, that in the presidential election of 1796, Burr received 30 electoral votes to 68 for Jefferson and 71 for the winner, John Adams. At that time, there were no party tickets for president and vice president as there are today. In the first presidential elections, several nominations were made and there was no campaigning.

John Adams was elected president in 1796.

The person who received the most electoral votes became president, the person who came in second was vice president. Thus, in 1796, the Federalist Adams became president and his political enemy, Thomas Jefferson, became vice president.

Despite receiving votes for president, Burr lost his Senate position to Philip Schuyler in 1796. He returned to his law practice in New York, but kept an active interest in politics. In 1797, he was elected to the New York state assembly and began making plans for a national position.

As the presidential election of 1800 drew near, Burr used his connections and his knowledge of politics to build a solid Republican base of support. For the second time, his name, along with that of

Jefferson, was put forth for president. Hamilton, a dedicated Federalist, supported Adams for re-election and did all he could to defeat Burr in New York. For the first time, negative campaigning—spreading gossip about a candidate—was used.

Thomas Jefferson became John Adams's vice president.

The popular vote for president in 1800 was overwhelmingly in favor of Jefferson. Burr, however, had carried New York and other thickly populated Northern states with many electoral votes. Thus, when the electoral college voted, the results showed 73 votes each for Burr and Jefferson. For the first time, an election was sent to the House of Representatives to be decided. Vote after vote was taken with no winner. Hamilton used all his powers to persuade lawmakers to choose

Jefferson. Ironically, Hamilton considered Jefferson a political enemy because of Jefferson's anti-Federalist beliefs. As much as he disliked Jefferson's politics, however, Hamilton had developed a personal hatred for Burr. He referred to Jefferson as "by far not so dangerous a man" as Burr. He said the Burr was "beyond redemption," and a man who "has nothing in his favor."

The unsettled election dragged on for more than 30 House ballots, or votes. Even though he knew that Jefferson had received many more popular votes, Burr refused to concede the election. Finally, Jefferson won on the 36th ballot. Burr became the vice president. After the confusion of the 1800 election, the Twelfth Amendment was added to the Constitution. This required voters and electors to cast separate votes for president and vice president.

Burr's refusal to concede the election cost him political influence. After the long drawn-out balloting and the attacks on Burr's character by Hamilton, Jefferson developed a deep mistrust of Burr. The new vice president, however, was good at his job. In his position, Burr was called upon to preside over the Senate during debates, and he was considered a

AARON BURR AND THE YOUNG NATION

master at this task. One senator said that Burr "states the question clearly and confines speakers to the point." He added that Burr presided with "great ease and dignity."

Jefferson, however, had made up his mind about his vice president. Instead of appointing Burr's supporters to government jobs in New York, Jefferson appointed Burr's rivals. He also excluded Burr from any participation in the enormous purchase of the Louisiana Territory from France in 1803. By the time 1804 arrived, it was obvious to Burr that he would not be renominated for office in a Republican administration.

At this point, early in the year, Burr decided that if he could not win national office, he would run for state office as governor. Yet New York was a strongly Federalist state. Burr decided to approach Federalist leaders and offer to change parties to run. Thus, in 1804, Burr, the Republican vice president of the United States, was also Burr, Federalist candidate for governor of New York.

Even more troubling than Burr's split loyalty was a dangerous plan that was developing with his knowledge. Many Federalists in New England hated

Jefferson's Republican policies so much that they hatched a plan to secede from the Union. Some plotters approached Burr and promised him political power if would deliver New York to the Federalist cause once he was elected. Burr made no such promises, but he did not alert anyone in the federal government about the plan either.

Even a committed Federalist like Hamilton was alarmed when he heard of the plans to secede. And the fact that Burr had not spoken out against the plotters gave Hamilton even more reason to hate his rival. Hamilton made several public comments about the "despicable" character of Aaron Burr. These comments, and the fact that Burr had switched parties while still holding office, led many New Yorkers to doubt Burr's honesty. As a result, in April 1804, Burr lost the general election to Republican Morgan Lewis by a landslide. This loss was largely the result of public attacks by George Clinton and DeWitt Clinton, the powerful New York Republicans who backed Lewis. Burr began to realize that his political career was finished. When he read a letter in an Albany newspaper that claimed Hamilton had referred to him as "despicable," Burr was enraged.

He felt that his only course of action was to write and demand that Hamilton retract his insults. This, Burr believed, would at least give him back his reputation, if not his political power. Hamilton, however, was bitter and unyielding on the matter. He refused to apologize. Hamilton said that he valued honesty above all other virtues, and to say that he was sorry for what he had called Burr would be dishonest. "I have not censured him on light grounds," Hamilton wrote of Burr. "I certainly have strong reasons for what I have said."

Burr now felt he had no choice. His honor had been attacked. As was the custom, he challenged Hamilton to a duel.

Dewitt Clinton helped defeat Burr in the New York gubernatorial election of 1804.

Early on July 11, 1804, the most famous duel in American history took place. The vice president of the United States and the first secretary of the treasury stood at ten paces. A Revolutionary War colonel faced off against a Revolutionary War general. Two of the most brilliant men in early American history pointed pistols at each other. But one man, Burr, did not know that the other, Hamilton, would waste his shot. Aaron Burr aimed and fired, killing Alexander Hamilton.

Chapter 6

"GLORY AND FORTUNE" THE CONSPIRACY

*I*n the days following Hamilton's death, religious leaders, politicians, and educators spoke out against the practice of dueling. In the wake of this tragedy, Aaron Burr became the most hated American leader since Benedict Arnold.

Burr was charged with murder in New York and New Jersey and fled south to Georgia for several weeks. Although dueling was frowned upon in the North, in the South it was considered an acceptable method for defending one's honor. And though Hamilton was a hero to many in the North, few Southerners had ever supported the Federalist Party or Hamilton.

Aaron Burr presided over the impeachment trial of Chief Justice Samuel Chase (pictured).

Eventually, Burr returned to Washington, D.C., to serve out the remainder of his term. He was immune from prosecution there and felt obligated to honor his commitment to the government. During his last few months, Burr presided over the impeachment trial of Samuel Chase, a justice of the U.S. Supreme Court. Despite his personal problems, Burr was at his best in such situations. He was praised for his fair handling of the trial in which Chase was acquitted by one vote—Burr's.

A Plot Takes Shape

Even during the Chase trial, however, Burr was planning a new direction for his life. The hostile treatment of the press—comparing him to Arnold, for example—may have pushed him to act against the nation. Whatever the reason,

Aaron Burr traveled down the Ohio River seeking support for his plan.

Burr decided that his future lay in the West, in the huge Louisiana Territory that had been acquired from France a year earlier. The land was mostly wilderness, and Burr came to believe that with a small, well-armed militia he could create his own nation in the Louisiana Territory. If that succeeded, Burr believed, he could lead his army further south into Mexico and take control of most or all of that country.

Burr shared these thoughts with his daughter, who had married several years earlier. Theodosia Burr Alston was bitterly angry with the treatment her father had received in the press after the Hamilton

Burr found a willing ally in Harman Blennerhassett, a wealthy Irishman.

duel. Aware that her father not only faced financial ruin, but was also politically powerless, she encouraged him to leave the East, head west, and build support for his plan.

Shortly after completing his term as vice president, Burr traveled to western territories including Pennsylvania and Ohio, which were mostly wilderness at the time. His goal was to see how much support he might receive for his idea. To his delight, he found enthusiastic listeners in many outposts along the frontier. Sailing along the Ohio River, Burr encountered one man, Harman Blennerhassett, who became convinced that Burr's plan could succeed.

Blennerhassett was an Irish nobleman who had come to America and traveled west with a family fortune. He had bought slaves and planned to live the life of plantation owner. Slavery was illegal in Ohio, however, so the wealthy Irishman built a small plantation on an island in the Ohio River—near the town of Marietta, but outside the jurisdiction of the state. As someone who viewed laws and government with disdain, Blennerhassett was a perfect ally for Burr. The two men talked of using the island as a staging area for Burr's army, and Blennerhasset volunteered to take on the job and much of the cost of raising the force. In return, Burr offered Blennerhassett the chance to rule part of his "empire."

General James Wilkinson, governor of the Northern Louisiana Territory, was one of Burr's co-conspirators.

With his plan taking shape, Burr had to begin to recruit soldiers and obtain weapons. For this, the brashly confident Burr sought out U.S. army general James Wilkinson, who was then serving as the governor of the Northern Louisiana territory. Burr had known Wilkinson since the two had served under Benedict Arnold in 1775. Though

Burr secretly considered Wilkinson a dishonest brag-gart, the two had become political allies at various times in their careers. And since Wilkinson was a governor, he could move forces anywhere in the territory without anyone challenging him.

With Blennerhassett on the Ohio River, and Wilkinson farther south along the Mississippi River, Burr had key allies in important positions. Before he left Wilkinson to complete his voyage down the river, Wilkinson gave him the names of several wealthy businessmen and politicians who might help the attempt with financial support. Burr sailed south down the river to New Orleans, spreading word of his plan at every stop along the way. In New Orleans, he met Wilkinson's contacts and convinced several prominent men that his dream could become reality.

By late 1805, Burr was back in Washington, great-ly encouraged. He knew, however, that to build a nation, he would have to establish alliances with for-eign powers. His first step, once he returned to the capital, was to contact a British diplomat stationed there and lay out his plot. The minister relayed Burr's offer, along with his request for money and

Burr traveled down the Mississippi River to New Orleans to recruit volunteers for his plan.

"GLORY AND FORTUNE"

THE CIPHER LETTER

There was perhaps no more convincing evidence—at least in the court of public opinion—of Burr's guilt than the coded letter he sent to General James Wilkinson in July 1806.

The letter, dictated by Burr and written by his private secretary, Willie, was composed in Philadelphia and carried by messenger to Wilkinson in Louisiana. After Burr's arrest, the prosecution tried to introduce the letter as evidence against Burr. Burr's secretary, Willie, was called to answer questions that would verify the letter. Defense attorneys argued that Willie's answers violated his Fifth Amendment rights against self-incrimination. Chief Justice John Marshall ruled that Willie could refuse to answer questions concerning his former knowledge of the contents of the letter, but must answer questions concerning his present knowledge of the contents—which was of no value to the prosecution since it could not establish the origin of the document. The decoded letter that appeared in national newspapers read:

"I have obtained funds, and have actually commenced the enterprise. Detachments from different points under different pretenses will rendezvous on the Ohio, 1st November— everything internal and external favors views—protection of England is secured. T[ruxton] is gone to Jamaica to arrange with the admiral on that station, and will meet at the Mississippi— England—-Navy of the United States are ready to join, and final orders are given to my friends and followers—it will be a host of choice spirits. Wilkinson shall be second to Burr only—Wilkinson shall dictate the rank and promotion of his officers. Burr will proceed westward 1st August, never to return: with him go his daughter—the husband will follow in October with a corps of worthies. Send forthwith an intelligent and confidential friend with whom Burr may confer. He shall return immediately with further interesting details—this is essential to concert and harmony of the movement.... [T]he project is brought to the point so long desired: Burr guarantees the result with his life and honor—the lives, the honor and fortunes of hundreds, the best blood of our country. Burr's plan of operations is to move rapidly from the falls on the 15th of November, with the first five hundred or one thousand men, in light boats now constructing for that purpose—to be at Natchez between the 5th and 15th of December—then to meet Wilkinson—then to determine whether it will be expedient in the first instance to seize on or pass by Baton Rouge. On receipt of this send Burr an answer—draw on Burr for all expenses, &c. The people of the country to which we are going are prepared to receive us— their agents now with Burr say that if we will protect their religion, and will not subject them to a foreign power, that in three weeks all will be settled.

The gods invite to glory and fortune—it remains to be seen whether we deserve the boon."

ships, to London. Even though the British were still bitter from the loss of their colonies, the plan's success seemed highly unlikely to British leaders. Nothing ever came of the contact.

Burr spent early 1806 gathering more recruits. He believed that he had the solid—but silent—support of many well-known politicians and businessmen. Those non-fighting recruits had been drawn into the plan by their own dreams of becoming wealthy landowners in Mexico.

By midyear, however, his supporters were not the only people who knew of Burr's intentions. The scheme was too big to conceal. Articles about Burr's plans had begun appearing in Eastern newspapers. Burr, however, remained confident in his plan and continued to seek support. As the summer of 1806 arrived, he was ready to begin his final push. To alert Wilkinson that the time had come, Burr sent the governor-general a letter outlining the final procedure. The letter, written in code, later became known as the "Cipher Letter."

In August, Burr left Pittsburgh and set sail down the Ohio River with his daughter and her 4-year-old child. His first stop was Blennerhassett's Island, where his new ally was building boats and securing provisions for Burr and his force. While Blennerhassett made preparations, Burr continued his recruiting, making trips along the Ohio River to areas around Ohio and Kentucky.

But even as Burr began his final moves, rumors about his plan were spreading. Because communication moved so slowly in those days, however, Burr was unaware that he was a marked man. By late 1806, Wilkinson had concluded that the plan would not work. He decided to save his career and sent a letter to President Jefferson describing the conspiracy without mentioning Burr. With newspapers filled with articles of Burr's misdeeds, however, Jefferson understood who the chief conspirator was.

Jefferson took immediate steps to stop his former vice president. On December 9, 1806, the Ohio militia captured some of Burr's supplies at a Marietta boatyard. On December 11, the militia invaded Blennerhassett's Island, destroying the plantation in the process. The government forces discovered that Blennerhassett himself, and most of the force, had already sailed downriver.

Blennerhassett met Burr on the southern Ohio River in late December. Burr, who expected a well-armed force of several thousand men saw fewer than 100 poorly equipped, untrained men. The end was near, but Burr did not give up. He continued south down the Mississippi, adding men to his pitifully small force at every port.

Burr was less than 30 miles from New Orleans when he realized that his plan had failed. Stopping to make camp, he was handed a newspaper with a front-page headline that offered a reward for his capture. The article contained the entire Cipher Letter he had sent to Wilkinson, decoded and printed for the public to read.

Burr surrendered and was taken before a grand jury. Using his legal skills, Burr explained that he had no intention of attacking any U.S. territory, and the jury refused to indict him. The judge, however, was not convinced of Burr's innocence and ordered Burr to appear before the court. Certain that he would be jailed, Burr fled.

His flight, however, was short-lived. On February 13, 1807, he was captured. In a bitter twist, the troops who captured him were commanded by General Wilkinson.

AARON BURR AND THE YOUNG NATION

BURR'S FLIGHT.

After a judge ordered him jailed,
Burr fled from authorities.

Accompanied by nine armed guards, the former vice president made a 1,000-mile trip on horseback to the federal court at Richmond, Virginia. He was charged with treason.

In a few short years, Burr had gone from national leader to killer to traitor. Few Americans in the public eye have fallen so far so fast. His trial in Richmond began in April 1807, with the convening of a grand jury. Witnesses were called to testify about conversations with Burr. A well-known Indian fighter, Colonel Daniel Morgan, testified about a dinner he had had with Burr in Pittsburgh:

"After dinner I spoke of our fine country. I observed that when I first went there, there was not a single family between the Allegheny mountains and the Ohio; and that by and by we should have congress sitting in this neighborhood or at Pittsburgh. We were allowed to sport these things over a glass of wine: 'No, never,' said Colonel Burr, 'for in less than five years you will be totally divided from the Atlantic states.' The colonel entered into some arguments to prove why it would and must be so....He said that our taxes were very heavy, and demanded why we should pay them to the Atlantic parts of the country?....I began to think that all was not right. He said that with two hundred men he could drive congress, with the president at its head, into the river Potomac, or that it might be done; and he said with five hundred men he could take possession of New York."

Evidence was also introduced that Burr had arranged the purchase of 15 boats capable of carrying 500 men, and a large keelboat for transporting supplies. He had placed orders for huge rations of pork, corn meal, flour, and whiskey.

Well-known Revolutionary general Daniel Morgan testified against Burr.

Finally, General Wilkinson appeared before the grand jury. The author Washington Irving, who attended the trial, wrote that Wilkinson "strutted into court" and "stood for a moment swelling like a turkey-cock." Then, wrote Irving, Burr "turned his head, looked him full in the face with one of his piercing regards, swept his eye over the whole person from head to foot, as if to scan his dimensions, and then coolly resumed his former position."

Wilkinson's testimony sealed Burr's fate before the grand jury. On June 24, the jury members indicted Burr for treason. Burr pleaded not guilty, and the court was adjourned until August 3.

The trial began much as the grand jury proceeding had. A witness testified to a conversation that he had in Washington with Burr during the winter of 1805-6:

"I listened as Colonel Burr now laid open his project of revolutionizing the territory west of the Allegheny, establishing an independent empire there; New Orleans to be the capital, and he himself to be the chief; organizing a military force on the waters of the Mississippi, and carrying conquest to Mexico."

Burr's treason trial began in Richmond, Virginia, in April 1807.

Other prosecution witnesses verified discussing with Burr his ambitious plans. Even Harman Blennerhassett's gardener testified to a conversation he had with Blennerhassett:

"He made a sudden pause, and said, 'I will tell you what, Peter, we are going to take Mexico, one of the finest and richest places in the whole world.' He said that Colonel Burr would be the king of Mexico, and Mrs. Alston, daughter of Colonel Burr, was to be the queen of Mexico whenever Colonel Burr died. He said that Colonel Burr had made fortunes for many in his time, but none for himself; but now he was going to make something for himself."

A Controversial Decision

On August 20, Burr rose during the prosecution's case to ask the court to declare his innocence because the evidence "utterly failed to prove any overt act of war had been committed." Burr also pointed out that he was shown to have been at least 100 miles south of Blennerhassett's Island at the time the militia captured the supplies and men. At this point, Chief Justice John Marshall praised lawyers on both sides, saying that their arguments had been made with "a degree of eloquence seldom displayed on any occasion."

Marshall then ruled that Burr could not have committed treason based on the events at Blennerhassett's Island simply because he was not there. He also pointed out that under the strict definition of treason in the Constitution, the prosecution had to prove that an actual act of treason had been committed by a defendant in a war. Under the Constitution, said Marshall, the act must be witnessed by two people and must have taken place in the district of the trial. Marshall's ruling ended the prosecution's case and left the jury little choice. Burr was declared not guilty.

Chief Justice John Marshall presided over Burr's treason trial.

The Aftermath

Jefferson was enraged by Marshall's ruling. He told newspaper reporters, "It now appears we have no law but the will of the judge." Ironically, the president, who was known as a champion of independence, even went so far as to propose a constitutional amendment limiting the power of the judiciary and asked Congress to impeach the chief justice. In a letter to General Wilkinson—who barely escaped indictment for treason himself—Jefferson wrote:

President Thomas Jefferson was outraged at Burr's acquittal.

"The scenes which have been acted at Richmond are such as have never been exhibited in any country, where all regard to public character has not yet been thrown off. They are equivalent to a proclamation of impunity to every traitorous combination which may be formed to destroy the Union."

Burr's innocence in the courtroom did not matter to the Americans who had learned of his plan. He was still considered by many to be someone who had gotten away with murder for the duel with Hamilton. Now, people complained, Burr had gotten away with treason. Burr realized that there was really no place in the United States where he was welcome. He had turned his back on his country, and now Americans turned their backs on him. In early 1808, Burr left for Europe, where he spent several years fruitlessly attempting to draw various British and French officials into plots to invade North America.

After four years, Burr returned to America. It was then that he suffered the worst tragedy of his life. His daughter, Theodosia, was sailing from South Carolina to New York City to greet her father's return when the ship was lost at sea. Burr was devastated. He wrote in his memoirs that he felt "severed from the human race."

Aaron Burr

Burr returned to a changed nation. By mid-1812, the United States was on the brink of war with Great Britain. With the nation newly preoccupied, Burr became the forgotten man that he is today. He simply opened a law office in New York City and solicited business. He lived another 24 years in obscurity, and died at age 80.

Shortly before his death in 1836, he learned that American settlers in the territory of Texas had declared their independence from Mexico to form a separate nation. He remarked to a colleague that he had simply been ahead of his time with his plans for an empire. (Burr would not be around to see the "nation" of Texas become a state in 1845.)

It is interesting to imagine what the United States might have looked like if Burr has succeeded in some of his plans. Had he been elected governor of New York in 1804, for example, he might have been effective in helping to split that state and New England from the rest of the Union. There was no army strong enough to hold the country together then. That was also true of the untamed land west of the Mississippi River. Had Burr succeeded in separating Louisiana from the

United States, the course of the young nation might have changed completely.

As it was, Aaron Burr became nothing more than a curious—but notorious—character in American history. The brilliant scholar, brave soldier, and skillful politician who dreamed of an empire died as a forgotten man. President Woodrow Wilson, also a Princeton graduate, described Aaron Burr as someone who had "genius enough to have made him immortal, and unschooled passion enough to make him infamous."

Chronology

The Life of Aaron Burr

February 6, 1756	Aaron Burr is born in Newark, New Jersey.
1759	Burr is orphaned.
1769	At the age of 13, Aaron Burr is accepted for advanced placement as a sophomore at Princeton.
1772	Aaron Burr graduates from college.
1775	In Cambridge, Massachusetts, 19-year-old Aaron Burr presents himself to George Washington, commander-in-chief of the Continental army. Burr asks for a commission, but Washington has none to spare. Burr joins Benedict Arnold's expedition to Canada.
1776	Burr is named to General Washington's staff as military secretary. But he and Washington do not get along, and Burr's tenure is brief.
1778	Burr commands regiment at the Battle of Monmouth, New Jersey.
1779	Burr retires from service and meets Theodosia Prevost.
1782.	Burr marries Theodosia Prevost. Aaron Burr is admitted to the New York bar in Albany.
1783	Aaron Burr's daughter, also named Theodosia, is born.
1784	Burr is elected to the New York State Assembly.
1791	Burr wins a U.S. Senate seat, defeating Philip Schuyler, Alexander Hamilton's father-in-law.
1794	Burr's wife dies.
1800	Burr and Thomas Jefferson receive an equal number of electoral votes for president. Congress votes to make Jefferson president.
1804	Burr loses election for governor of New York, largely due to remarks made by Hamilton during the campaign. Anxious to repair his failing career, Burr challenges Hamilton to a duel. Hamilton reluctantly accepts the challenge.

July 11, 1804	Hamilton and Burr duel in Weehawken, New Jersey. Each fires a shot. Hamilton suffers a mortal wound and dies the next day.
Feb. 4- Mar. 1, 1805	In his final act as vice president, Burr presides over the impeachment trial of Judge Samuel Chase.
April 30, 1805	Burr sets off down the Ohio River from Pittsburgh.
May 5, 1805	Burr lands on Blennerhassett Island and stays with Harman Blennerhassett.
June 1805	Burr meets with General James Wilkinson. Wilkinson gives Burr letters of introduction to wealthy friends in New Orleans.
July 29, 1806	Burr sends a letter in coded language to Wilkinson saying he has "commenced the enterprise."
August 1806	Burr, his daughter, and his granddaughter begin a trip down the Ohio River.
September 1806	On Blennerhassett Island, Burr draws up an agreement with Blennerhassett for boats, recruits, and supplies. He travels through Ohio, Kentucky, and Tennessee, seeking more recruits.
October 1806	Wilkinson decides to oppose Burr and sends a message to President Jefferson detailing Burr's plan.
December 1806	The Ohio militia attacks Blennerhassett Island.
Late January 1807	Burr is captured. He escapes, but is recaptured and taken to Richmond, Virginia.
August 3, 1807	Burr's trial opens.
Sept. 1, 1807	Burr is found not guilty of treason.
1812	Burr returns to the United States after several years in Europe. His daughter is lost at sea and presumed dead.
1836	Burr dies in New York City.

The History of a Nation

1756	The Seven Years' War, called the French and Indian War in the British colonies, begins.
1763	England wins the Seven Years' War.

1765	Parliament passes the Stamp Act.
1770	British troops fire on American civilians in what becomes known as the "Boston Massacre."
April 19, 1775	Colonists fight British troops at Lexington and Concord.
July 4, 1776	The Declaration of Independence is signed.
Winter 1777-1778	Continental army spends a brutal winter at Valley Forge.
June 1778	Americans defeat the British at the Battle of Monmouth.
October 19, 1781	Americans win the Battle of Yorktown, ending the American Revolution.
1787	Delegates attend the Constitutional Convention.
1789	George Washington takes office as the first president of the United States.
1803	The Louisiana Purchase doubles the size of the United States.
1812	The United States goes to war with Great Britain.

Glossary

Duel An arranged armed contest between two rivals performed before witnesses.

Militia Citizen soldiers with little discipline or training who served in town and state units during the Revolutionary War.

Minutemen Militia men ready to fight the British at a moment's notice.

Notorious Widely and unfavorably known.

Rival Opponent, enemy.

Villain A person blamed for a particular evil or wrongdoing.

Source Notes

Chapter 1

Page 8:   "unprincipled . . ." and "beyond redemption . . ." Quoted in Joseph Ellis, *Founding Brothers*. New York: Alfred A. Knopf, 2001, p. 42.

Page 9:   "ill will . . ." Quoted in Ellis, *Founding Brothers*, p. 23.

Page 12:   "throw away my first fire . . ." Quoted in Ellis, *Founding Brothers*, p. 23.

Pages 12-13:   "This is a mortal wound . . ." Quoted in Ellis, *Founding Brothers*, p. 25.

Page 14:   "the most dramatic moment in the early politics of the Union . . ." Quoted in quoted in Ellis, *Founding Brothers*, p. 40.

Page 15:   "O, Burr, O, Burr, what hast thou done? . . ." Quoted in Ellis, *Founding Brothers*, p. 27.

Chapter 2

Page 23:   "dirty, noisy boy, sly and mischievous . . ." Quoted in *A Hypertext on American History: From the Colonial Period until Modern Times*. http://odur.let.rug.nl/~usa/B/aburr/burr.htm.

Page 23:   "beaten like a sack . . ." Quoted in *A Hypertext on American History*.

Chapter 3

Page 31:   "taxation without representation . . ." Quoted in Daniel Boorstin. *A History of the United States*. Lexington, MA: Ginn and Company, 1981, p. 72.

Chapter 4

Page 50::   "She had the truest heart and finest intellect . . ." Quoted in *A Hypertext on American History*.

Chapter 5

Page 71:   "Unprincipled . . ." and "if he can . . ." Quoted in Ellis, *Founding Brothers*, p. 42.

Page 76:   "by far not so dangerous . . ." Quoted in Ellis, *Founding Brothers*, p. 42.

Page 76:   "beyond redemption . . ." and "nothing in his favor . . ." Quoted in Ellis, *Founding Brothers*, p. 42.

Page 77:   "states the question clearly and confines speakers to the point . . ." Quoted in *A Hypertext on American History*.

Page 77: "great ease and dignity . . ." Quoted in *A Hypertext on American History*.

Page 78:: "despicable . . ." Quoted in Ellis, *Founding Brothers*, p. 32.

Page 78: "I have not censured him on light grounds . . ." Quoted in Ellis, *Founding Brothers*, p. 38.

Chapter 6

Page 95: "After dinner I spoke . . ." Quoted in Douglas Linder, *Famous American Trials: The Aaron Burr Trial 1807*. www.law.umkc.edu/faculty/projects/ftrials/burr/burrtrial.html.

Page 97: "strutted into court . . ." Quoted in Linder, *Famous American Trials*.

Page 97: "I listened as Colonel Burr . . ." Quoted in Linder, *Famous American Trials*.

Page 98:: "He made a sudden pause . . ." Quoted in Linder, *Famous American Trials*.

Page 99: "a degree of eloquence . . ." Quoted in Linder, *Famous American Trials*.

Page 100: "It now appears . . ." Quoted in Linder, *Famous American Trials*.

Page 102 "severed from the human race . . ." Quoted in "The Duel," Mark Steele, ed., *The American Experience*. www.pbs.org/wgbh/amex/duel/filmmore/ description.html.

Page 103: "genius enough . . ." Quoted in *A Hypertext on American History*.

Further Reading

Gaines, Ann Graham. *The Louisiana Purchase in American History.* In American History. Berkeley Heights, NJ: Enslow Publishers, 2000.

Haesly, Richard. *The Constitutional Convention, History Firsthand.* San Diego: Greenhaven Press, Inc., 2001.

Jones, Veda Boyd. *Thomas Jefferson: Author of the Declaration of Independence.* Broomall, PA: Chelsea House, 2000.

Miller, Susan. *The Boston Massacre.* American Adventure. Broomall, PA: Chelsea House, 2000.

Nardo, Don. *The Declaration of Independence: A Model for Individual Rights.* Words that Changed History. San Diego: Lucent Books, 1999.

Rosenburg, John M. *Alexander Hamilton: America's Bold Lion.* Breckenridge, CO: Twenty First Century Books, 2000.

Smolinski, Diane. *Land Battles of the Revolutionary War.* Americans at War. Portsmouth, NH: Heinemann, 2001.

Whitelaw, Nancy. *The Shot Heard Round the World: The Battle of Lexington and Concord.* First Battles. Greensboro, NC: Morgan Reynolds, 2001.

Wise, William. *Aaron Burr.* Campbell, CA: Universe.com, 2001.

Web Sites

The American Presidency: Aaron Burr
http://gi.grolier.com/presidents/ea/vp/vpburr.html

American Memory, Library of Congress
http://lcweb2.loc.gov/ammem/bdsds/bdsdhome.html

America at War: American Military History: Revolutionary War to World War II
www.semo.net/suburb/dlswoff/amrev_p2.html

Sugar and Stamp Act
http://odur.let.rug.nl/~usa/E/sugar_stamp/actxx.htm

National Archives and Records Administration: The Declaration of Independence
www.nara.gov/exhall/charters/declaration/decmain.html

Battles of the Revolutionary War
www.ilt.columbia.edu/k12/history/aha/ARbattles.html

An Outline of American History
http://odur.let.rug.nl/~usa/H/1990/chap1.htm

Index